GW00792225

Driving to J

Driving to Nirvana

A Woman's Path
for Drivers
Without Cellular Phones

Clarice Bryan

NICOLAS-HAYS, INC.
York Beach, Maine

First published in 1997 by
Nicolas-Hays, Inc.
P. O. Box 612
York Beach, ME 03910-0612

Distributed to the trade by
Samuel Weiser, Inc.
P. O. Box 612
York Beach, ME 03910-0612

Library of Congress Cataloging-in-Publication Data

Bryan, Clarice.
    Driving to nirvana : a woman's path for drivers without
cellular phones / Clarice Bryan.
        p. cm.
    Includes bibliographical references (p.).
    ISBN 0-89254-037-0 (paper : alk. paper)
    1. Automobile driving--Psychological aspects. 2. Women
automobile drivers. 3. Meditation--Buddhism. I. Title.
TL152.5.Z56 1997
629.28'3'019--dc21   97-7259
                                                              CIP

ISBN 0-89254-037-0
MG
Cover art by Vera Bryan James, author's collection
Chinese characters on pages xiv, 18, 38, 50, 56, 60, 76, 82, and 88
by Dr. Lumei Hui
Cover and text design by Kathryn Sky-Peck
Typeset in Adobe Caslon with Nadianne display

Printed in the United States of America
03   02   01   00   99   98   97
10   9   8   7   6   5   4   3   2   1
*The paper used in this publication meets the minimum requirements of the
American National Standard for Permanence of Paper
for Printed Library Materials Z39.48-1984.*

This book is dedicated to my mother, Clarice Davis, who taught me to love driving, and to my grandmother, Leela Bryan, who taught my mother to love living.

Contents

Acknowledgments

My present moment, and this now past book have had many influences other than my foreparents and my genetic history. In particular, I would like to thank my friends who have helped me in this project in many ways: Kathryn Corbett, Patsy Givins, Gael Hodgkins, Jan Meninga, Dr. Rosalind Novic, Dr. Lumei Hui, Lynn Warner, Dr. Louise Watson, Phyllis Wilner, Dr. Lan Sing Wu, and, most recently, my publisher, Betty Lundsted.

Many authors and teachers are quoted in this book, and these precious quotes come from the following works: *page iii*: Zen Master Dogen, "Actualizing the Fundamental Point," in *Moon in a Dewdrop*, Kazuaki Tanahashi, ed. (San Francisco: North Point Press, 1985), p. 7; *page xviii*: Matthew Fox, *Creation Spirituality* (San Francisco: HarperSanFrancisco, 1991), p. 29; *page 1*: Pema Chodron, *Start Where You Are: A Guide to Compassionate Living* (Boston: Shambhala, 1994), p. 37;

page 5: Jane Wagner, *The Search for Signs of Intelligence in the Universe* (New York: HarperCollins, 1991), p. 18; *page 7*: Joan Ryan, "A Shortcut to Enlightenment," San Francisco Chronicle, November 24, 1996; *page 11*: Pema Chodron, *Start Where You Are: A Guide to Compassionate Living* (Boston: Shambhala, 1994), p. 4; *page 13*: Long Chen Pa, Tibetan Meditation Master, from a saying on a decorative poster; *page 17*: Wes "Scoop" Nisker, *Crazy Wisdom: The Saint, The Zen Master, The Poet, The Fool* (Berkeley: Ten Speed Press, 1990), p. 17; *page 19*: Robert Frost, "Forgive, O Lord..." in *Robert Frost Poetry and Prose*, Edward C. Lathem and Lawrence Thompson, eds. (New York: Holt, Rinehart and Winston, 1972), p. 171; *page 24*: Pema Chodron, *Start Where You Are: A Guide to Compassionate Living* (Boston: Shambhala, 1994), p. 7; *page 25*: Rachel Carson, *A Sense of Wonder* (New York: Harper & Row, 1956), p. 42; *page 32*: The Dalai Lama, *My Tibet* (Berkeley, CA: University of California Press, 1990), p. 109; *page 33*: Thich Nhat Hanh, *Peace is Every Step* (New York: Bantam, 1991), p. 32; *page 37*: Dhyani Ywahoo, in Sandy Boucher, *Turning the Wheel: American Women Creating the New Buddhism* (San Francisco: HarperSanFrancisco, 1988), p. 170; *page 39*: Matthew Fox, *Creation Spirituality* (San Francisco: HarperSanFrancisco, 1991), p. 128; *page 44*: Albert Schweitzer, *The Wisdom of Albert Schweitzer* (New York:

Philosophical Library, 1968), p. 58; *page 45*: Charlotte Joko Beck, *Everyday Zen: Love and Work* (San Francisco: HarperSanFrancisco, 1989), p. v; *page 49*: Thich Nhat Hanh, *Peace is Every Step* (New York: Bantam, 1991), p. 21; *page 51*: The Dalai Lama, *My Tibet* (Berkeley, CA: University of California Press, 1990), p. 108; *page 55*: The Dalai Lama, *My Tibet*, p. 107; *page 57*: Carlos Fuentes. Honnold Lecture given at Knox College, Galesburg, IL. Knox Alumnus 7, October 14, 1981; *page 62*: Alan Watts, *The Wisdom of Insecurity* (New York: Vintage, 1951), p. 116; *page 63*: Thich Nhat Hanh, *Peace is Every Step* (New York: Bantam, 1991), p. 34; *page 68*: Alan Watts, *Nature, Man, and Woman* (New York: Vintage Books, 1970), p. 122- 123; *page 71*: Alan Watts, *The Wisdom of Insecurity* (New York: Vintage, 1951), p. 125; *page 75*: Wes "Scoop" Nisker, *Crazy Wisdom* (Berkeley, CA: Ten Speed Press, 1990), p. 48; *page 77*: Alan Watts, *The Book* (New York: Vintage, 1966), p. 129; *page 81*: Alan Watts, *The Book*, pp. 129-130; *page 83*: Matthew Fox, *Creation Spirituality* (San Francisco: HarperSanFrancisco, 1991), p. 12; *page 87*: Alan Watts, *The Wisdom of Insecurity* (New York: Vintage, 1951), p. 116.

Introduction

To study Buddhism is to study ourselves, to study ourselves is to forget ourselves.

—Zen Master Dogen

Mindfulness.

*T*his small volume makes no attempt to be a scholarly treatise on Buddhism in the ordinary sense. It is experience and mindfulness, lived and living, as applied to driving, from a woman Buddhist's point of view.

I have traveled from Methodism to Atheism, from Pantheism to my present form of Buddhism. What next, I don't know yet.

I do know that every time I drive to The City, I am amazed at the naivete of our drivers. It seems like a miracle that so many of us make it unscathed to the end of the day. Nirvana can be achieved in everyday life through many different paths. This is just one application. Women get less help in the art of driving than men, so my focus is for women.

It has been a hundred years since people started driving cars. Initially, the thought of a woman driving a motorcar was considered a joke at best and impossible at worst. Women's indecisiveness, timidity, weakness, and ignorance of mechanics led most women as well as men to believe that motorcars were for men only.

After The Great War and Women's Suffrage, the notion about gender roles started to dislocate a little. Economic competition and technological advances created markets for motorcars, and in a few decades, women seized the opportunity and women drivers became commonplace. Women were no longer just passive passengers. They had invaded the male turf of the motor world and loved it. There was now a market for women drivers.

The American auto industry created a car-buying public, and our cultural geography was changed forever. Design and marketing strategies made cars available to many elements of the changing social profile, transforming American life. Driving has become essential to our economy and way of life for women as much as for men. We are a car culture.

Driving can be hazardous to your health. As time concerns increasingly drive us to do everything as fast as possible, it is no wonder that our highways have become potential explosions and cars have become lethal weapons. It is no fun to play a game where people are driven by ego, territory, aggressiveness and separateness. Some of us react to cars with a sense of power and mastery. The car yields to our will and emotions, providing autonomy and independence. Driving the car brings an enlargement of life and our ability to manipulate life.

But, power and independence are an illusion. Better if we all participate harmoniously together in our life on the road, where we are all on the same team. We can use our capabilities in interaction and cooperation because we are interconnected, merging and separating at various angles, but still flowing down the same moving stream.

As a player and a teacher it has been wonderful to experience everyone as a teammate with no real opponents and everyone striving for the same goal—excellence. There are not too many games like that. It is not always easy to get into a harmonious driving game, but it is possible and it is worth it.

Nirvana is a state in which one has overcome desire, hatred, and delusion, and has arrived at the unified nature of the world. It involves transcendence over ego and selfishness leading to the ultimate unity with the absolute.

Nirvana is another mode of existence which is beyond speech and thought, where there are no words to express the feeling of fulfillment, ecstacy, awe, innocence, arrival, and understanding of the essence of life.

In driving, as all other things, there is only awareness and experience, ever changing, never the same.

There are no rules except to be as mindful, as aware and as single-minded about your driving as possible, feeling yourself as your car and feeling all the other cars around you as part of the ebb and flow of the stream of traffic. Like water in a stream or a rushing river you dance to the rhythms of the pebbles on the bottom and the boulders pushing up along the way.

You become driving. There are no other thoughts or worries to separate yourself from driving.

A path is a way of solidarity, of sharing the beauty with all the others on the way; it is also a sharing of the pain and the struggle with all the others on the way.

—MATTHEW FOX

1

Waving

*By the same token, if you feel some sense of
delight. . . if you connect with what for you is
inspiring, opening, relieving, relaxing . . . you
breathe it out, you give it away, you send it out
to everyone else.*

—PEMA CHODRON

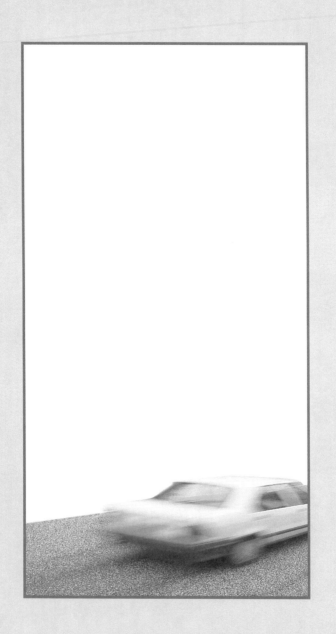

I have always been a fast driver, a fast walker, a person who wastes no time. But, in later years I can see that I have changed a bit. I can remember when I drove as fast as sanity would allow, in and out of lanes, sparing no space, racing ahead of anyone out there with me. Faster and faster. Never hesitating. My concentration was so involved in passing other cars, that I could not tell what was playing on the radio or if there were trees along the roadside, or houses, or deserts.

Then, one day, it happened. About twenty-five years ago, I was driving on a two-lane highway in Humboldt County, racing along at a pretty good clip on a curvey section of the road, and some jerk had the audacity to race up to me from behind and sit on my bumper. I did not like this. If anything, I was more apt to be the one doing such a thing. I speeded up and no matter how fast I went, he stuck to my bumper. I was going excessively fast, even for me. He had no right to want to go faster! But, apparently, he believed he had the right to

Women drivers.

go faster. He did not toot his horn or blink his lights. He just stuck to my rear bumper without any breathing space.

It finally occurred to me that I would be much more comfortable if I could get him past me, no matter how obnoxious I found his behavior. I did not want to reward him for such rudeness, but a wide spot appeared in the road and I did the only thing I could do for my own sanity. I slowed and pulled into the wide spot and let him pass. Giving another the opportunity to pass me is something of a miracle all by itself, but there is even more. As he drove by, he waved at me. He waved at me!!! I was thrilled. I had done something for another person and he acknowledged it. I felt wonderful. I felt like a hero. I felt like I had pulled a tiny child from a burning building. I was a decent human being.

This was my first glimpse of the top of the mountain and I never had any idea that such a place existed.

Most of us suffer from the sensation that we are separate and self-contained, confronting the external world of people and things without any awareness that we are all results of the energy and development of our planet and universe. Most of us believe we are isolated in our own space bubbles where we can keep the world out as something separate and unpredictable. We tend to feel hostility and uncertainty toward everything outside our own skin. But beyond our skin is stuff of the same origin as the stuff inside our skin.

As long as there is a consciousness that is aware of having the experience, the moment is not all in the present. It is tangled up with observing rather than participating.

Reality is the leading cause of stress amongst those in touch with it.

—JANE WAGNER

Men drivers!

2

Connection

*Forget the trip to the Himalayas. Every
challenge a Buddhist monk could want can be
found in the life of a parent. But, then,
how would a monk know that?*

—JOAN RYAN

$\mathcal{I}$ began to love mountainous roads, even though they meant going slower. I smiled and felt wonderful at every opportunity to pull over for someone else. And, of course, I waved and sometimes gave a little toot when someone pulled out of the way for me. I began to feel a connection with other drivers. I even began to understand some of their needs. Often a pokey driver would be uncomfortable if I followed too close, so I would back off. But not so far that I couldn't pass if the opportunity arose. I was still a time-consumed person.

I found myself cooperating with other drivers—getting out of their way if they were too close to the center line, being patient when they were driving a motor home, becoming aware of their little quirks of slowing down for curves or speeding up on the straightaways, even when I was trying to pass. In most cases I decided that that was their way of trying to help me go faster. Not too effective, since, had they slowed on the straight I could have gotten around, but not mean, as I might have thought earlier in my life.

The competition that I used to feel was fading away. I became a master cooperator. I wanted to make people comfortable with my presence on the road. I wanted them to feel good about their own driving and about sharing the road with me.

And I began to feel there were no opponents, that we were all on the same team. We were all interrelated and no longer separate. I saw an image of us all moving together as if trying to reach the same goal in unison.

I loved the ebb and flow of our intermingling with each other in loving ways. Although we didn't actually touch, I could feel contact with the other drivers. I felt a sense of belonging whenever I had the opportunity to connect with my driving teammates.

We are all interconnected yet constantly changing and flowing. There is no separate self. All is everything. Nothing can exist without everything. We resonate with our environment and fellow travelers, often exchanging rhythm, music, intensity, or dance steps with each other.

Sensitivity and vitality require a high degree of delicacy and fragility, as we seek the ultimate degree of precision in our interrelationships.

Compassion toward others can only come from compassion toward oneself.

The reason we're often not there for others . . .
whether for our child or our mother or someone
who is insulting us or someone who frightens
us . . . is that we're not there for ourselves.

—PEMA CHODRON

.

3

Courtesy

*Since everything is but an apparition, perfect in
being what it is, having nothing to do with
good or bad, acceptance or rejection, one may
burst out in laughter.*

—LONG CHEN PA

Early in my career, I spent two years working in France. I knew I would never have enough money in my lifetime to feel I could afford what a trip to Europe would cost, so I worked for the government while I toodled around all those European countries on weekends.

French people love to drive fast and close, especially in downtown, clogged traffic and rush hours. I loved every minute of it. The French are not noted for their politeness and courtesy. They are too involved in the fast and furious speed with which they can zip around an étoile and flit out the other side, to be interested in anyone else's comfort or consideration. In spite of this, they were team players and worked hard at missing other cars, if only by inches.

Two years later, I came home and found that some things had changed in my own country. Some things were happening that I did not expect. Drivers were stopping for pedestrians! I almost rear-ended several cars until I finally adjusted to the idea as I learned this new tribal custom. It was a pleasant change. Pedestrians would smile and wave, and I would smile and wave back. It made the world closer and more comfortable.

But it could be overdone.

I was parking to go into a restaurant when I noticed a woman at an intersection stop her car for a pedestrian a half a block away, walking toward the corner. The driver could easily have driven off without causing the pedestrian to slow down in the slightest. But she stopped and almost got rear-ended herself. As the driver waved to the pedestrian to cross the street, the pedestrian smiled and waved and crossed. After the driver had departed, the pedestrian retraced his steps back across the street and turned the corner in another direction.

This kind of thing must have driven some drivers absolutely crazy. Often they honked rudely at the gracious driver who had stopped for someone. Unfortunately, this act of consideration for pedestrians no longer exists to any great extent in the larger cities. Our society seems to be rushing more and more so we can stop and wait at the next stop signal. Time is more important than people.

Every moment is here and now. This is the only moment in which we actually exist. Finding peace and love in ourselves right now, here, is being alive in the present moment. If we don't find it here, where will we find it? Tomorrow is another bunch of heres and nows which we must learn to live in today.

Complete awareness of the present, one moment at a time, without evaluating and comparing is the eternal present.

If we concentrate, we can live in happiness in the present.

Even the physicists have "proved" that reality depends on the observer. Revelation, like everything else, is in the eyes of the beholder.

—WES "SCOOP" NISKER

Get the binoculars out, honey. There's one way
back there that looks like a police car.

4

Sleepiness

Forgive, O Lord, my little jokes on thee
And I'll forgive thy great big one on me.

—ROBERT FROST

On long trips, I would sometimes get sleepy. Sometimes I would turn on the radio. Sometimes I would open the window. Sometimes I would turn on the air conditioner. Anything to keep from being too comfortable.

One time, when my eyes seemed to keep crossing and going out of focus, I woke up on the shoulder of the road about to veer off through a barbed wire fence and into a field. The roughness of the shoulder probably brought me back to my senses, so I straightened the car out and got back onto the road. But I was very scared— so scared that I woke right up, and didn't get sleepy while driving for a year or two.

But, on another occasion, my eyes started crossing and I thought I had enough will power to keep myself awake. Once again I woke up as the car bounced over a ditch and just missed a tree and a deep ravine. So much for will power.

My doctor says my hearing's gone and I can't see very well, but, at least I can still drive.

The best solution I have found for this problem is to pull over and take a nap. I carry an alarm clock in the glove compartment so that I can sleep soundly and without worry about waking up in time. I don't like to nap by the side of a noisy road, so I usually try to get to some town where there is a big enough store to have a parking lot with some empty spaces away from traffic.

Such parking lots are not always right around the next bend in the road. Sometimes the next town won't appear for 30 to 40 minutes. One time, while trying to stay awake until I could get to my next napping place, I started to sing some of the old songs. Romantic songs I used to sing when I was a dippy high school kid, or themes from movies that had reached my heart, or camp songs I'd learned at Scout Camp. Sometimes when I got to the next napping place I was wide awake and just kept on going.

There are some dangers to all this, however. Just last week when I was returning home from a trip to San Francisco, I started getting sleepy a little north of Santa Rosa. My next favorite napping place wasn't until Cloverdale, about 30 more minutes ahead. I started singing some old Nelson Eddy-Jeannette MacDonald songs.

I was straining away at a song called "My Hero" when I finally noticed the police car in my rearview mirror. And then his lights started blinking. And, of course, I pulled over.

"Well, you caught me singing," I said to the CHP officer. "You must have hit a few high notes," he said, "You were doing eighty!"

Our bodies are such miracles. We have eyes that sense movement, light, color, and shape. We have ears that can hear symphonies or thunderstorms. We can pirouette and arabesque around the dining room table and not even kick the cat. Our brains can analyze the properties of the atom, a speck of dust, or the architecture of Chartres. Yet, humans are fairly simple organisms when compared to the even more miraculous patterns of the environment, with such things as gravitational fields, electro-chemical interactions, photosynthesis, and the myriad of life forces.

The Lojong teachings encourage us, if we enjoy what we are experiencing, to think of other people and wish for them to feel the same way. Share the wealth.

—PEMA CHODRON

5

Beginners

*A child's world is fresh and new and beautiful,
full of wonder and excitement. It is our
misfortune that for most of us that clear-eyed
vision, that true instinct of what is beautiful and
awe-inspiring is dimmed and even lost before we
reach adulthood.*

—RACHEL CARSON

I grew up in a family of two parents, one grandmother, three siblings, and six cars. Yes, six. Sometimes more, but usually six cars.

We had so many cars because they were old, and we were always going to help one another when one of the cars broke down.

The very oldest car was a 1918 Dodge truck which rarely ran, but was a great hit with car buffs when it did. The next oldest was a '22 Dodge touring car with the top missing ever since my Dad had an accident in it. When I was very small the main family car was a '27 Dodge sedan, but by the time I was in high school we also had a '36 Dodge sedan. During the war we acquired a '37 Packard that needed two doors and two fenders which my Dad bought in junkyards and attached to the car. We also had a '36 Dodge truck that ran some of the time. Those are the main ones I remember, though there were others.

The best car we had while my Dad was still alive was a '29 Cadillac funeral car. This was the kind the bereaved family rode in to the cemetery. It was black on the outside, with gray velvet upholstery on the inside and had silver-plated door and window handles, and a roll-up window between the driver's seat and the real people in back. It had a set of jump seats facing backward toward the real people that could be opened up so the whole car could seat nine people comfortably.

Dad never believed in buying anything new, so most of these cars were at least ten years old when they entered the family.

Our home originally had a two-car garage so Dad and my brothers built another garage on the side of the original one, and later added garage space for two more cars in the driveway. There was still driveway space for three more cars but it never got turned into more garages.

My Dad rarely drove, and fortunately so. When he did drive, he went about 25 mph whether in traffic or highway and never stopped at stop signs. I don't think he liked to shift. So, my mother was the main driver, and she loved it, and was good at it.

A year or so after my Dad died, and Mom had disposed of all the old cars, she bought a BRAND NEW Ford. She and I were driving to Santa Cruz one day on the Bayshore Freeway, talking about the old days. I just happened to look at the speedometer and let out a loud "MOTHER, you're doing ninety!!!"

"My, my," she said. "I'm so used to the motor knocking when we get to fifty. I had no idea."

So, you see, it runs in the family.

My brother, Harry, who was six years older than I, often did things with me when I was growing up—like the dishes, or gardening, or painting projects, and we often sang while we did these things. He usually made a game out of what we were doing, so we would always try to do things a little faster and better than we had done them before.

I was the family ironer, so Harry taught me to iron faster and better every time I did it, aiming for all the weekly ironing to be done in five minutes! I never did make that, but he and I held a record for changing tires of two minutes flat. Not bad for those old cars with very strange jacks.

Harry believed that all the work would turn to play, and that is what we aimed for. Most of the time it WAS play! I was a very fortunate kid.

In our later years, we both changed somewhat, and found that just doing things better, not necessarily faster, was important in itself.

It's hard to believe it now, but I was a beginning driver once. In those days a person could get a special license at 14 if s/he needed it to drive to school or work, so I was lucky enough to drive a little sooner than people do now. And I loved it. Of course, driving is one of our first rites of adulthood. And responsibility. I became the chief errand-runner for most family chores.

But, as a beginner, I was often too slow in shifting, or I shifted while turning, or I didn't pay attention at an intersection, and didn't know whose turn it was to cross. Sometimes I drove too fast and jerkily, or didn't signal. Sometimes I braked too hard and shook up the people in the car. Sometimes I followed too close. Sometimes I looked too long at roadside attractions and veered off the road a little. Sometimes I made my grandmother seasick.

And sometimes I would get angry when people did unexpected things. I have had a tendency to think of erratic drivers as people who are inconsiderate jerks who ought to know better and who are just being mean. Well, this is not very calming for my stomach.

Now, I think of erratic drivers as beginners, and I don't get angry—I get patient. And, of course, many of them ARE beginners.

But, there are drivers out there that I do not want to have close to me. Some wobble from lane to lane, some jerk spasmodically when another car gets within twenty feet of them. I don't mind risk-takers as long as they don't threaten someone else. Maybe we should have race tracks for them to raise their endorphin levels or extinguish themselves in a fitting manner at no one else's expense.

We were all beginners once, in everything we have done. Sometimes we avoid doing things when we are beginners because taking that first step can be embarrassing. We all want to be experts without working at it. But most first steps lead to second steps, and if we are lucky we begin to climb to the top of the mountain. You don't get to the top of the mountain if you don't take that first step. It takes time and experience to grow into that state of mind that allows the rest to unify and become part of the being.

We can enjoy music without knowing either how it is written or how the body hears it. To know reality you cannot stand outside it and define it. You must be it and feel it, as an undivided entity.

When we are dancing we just float round and round with no intent to get across the dance floor before anyone else, or to be the best dancer on the floor. We just dance, fulfilled in each moment. The rhythm playing on our bodies and the music in our ears creates the pattern of the universe.

If we ourselves remain always angry and then
sing world peace, it has little meaning. So, you
see, first our individual self must learn peace.
This we can practice. Then we can teach
the rest of the world.

—THE DALAI LAMA

6

My Body the Car

When we use any instrument or machine we change. A violinist with his violin becomes very beautiful. A man with a gun becomes very dangerous. When we use a car, we are ourselves AND the car.

—THICH NHAT HANH

*I*t took me a long time to learn to control my body as a small child. It took a long time to keep from spilling my milk. It took a long time to learn to walk without falling down. It took a long time to keep from bumping into people when I was trying to go fast. And when I grew older, it took a long time for me to learn to draw well enough for others to recognize what I was drawing. It took a long time to learn to control my body and my speed to keep from bumping into people in basketball. It took a long time to learn to hit a tennis ball over the net but not over the fence.

And then I found myself seated in this huge suit of metal armor trying to figure out where the bumpers were, how far out the fenders went, if I was going to hit that car coming toward me or if he was in his own lane. It took a long time to fit into a diagonal parking space, let alone a parallel one. It took a long time to drive into a car wash and get my tires exactly in line with the tire grabber.

Extending my body image to include this hulking metal muumuu involved many first steps. It involved going slowly and learning control, which kept the dents in the bumpers and fenders to very small sizes, often not noticeable by parents with failing eyesight. With much practice I managed to keep this behemoth between two narrow lines and away from others of similar colossal size. And as I got better and better at fitting my walrus shape in and out of small oscillations of space that appeared on the horizon, I began to feel a sense of mastery and joy at my accomplishments.

And, finally, now I am the car! I have a kinesthetic awareness of where all my boundaries are, how much space I take up, which holes and spaces I can fit into. Sometimes I can feel the road ahead and around the corner as part of sensing my interrelatedness to everything.

It is not all honey and roses, however. When I first drove our new 4x4 three-quarter ton truck, I had to start as a beginner again. My whole body concept had changed. I thought I was as big as an eighteen-wheeler. A few practices in an empty parking lot helped a lot.

It becomes more and more difficult to draw a clear boundary between any one thing/person and its environment. Apart from our environment we do not exist. We are nothing. The human being is not an assemblage of parts as a car is. We don't come with a torso on which to attach legs, arms, and head. All of our being is developed together, and in harmony with our environment. We grow everything simultaneously and interdependently.

Differentiation and complexity do not mean separation. The brain and heart and liver tissue differentiate from the skin and muscle and connective tissue to perform necessary life functions, but nothing is separate from anything else.

People who are looking at art, people who are looking at the synergy of thought and action are more open to realizing the changing of the guard, and more willing to change forms; the issue is one's mind in a process of transition and seeing the world around in a process of transition.

—DHYANI YWAHOO

*I don't know what "right of way" means, so I'll
just stay here until everyone else has gone
through the intersection.*

Why is everyone always honking nowadays?

Interview

Creation is all things and us. It is us in relationship with all things.

—MATTHEW FOX

$\mathcal{I}$ had just finished an interview for a new job in San Francisco and felt pretty good about the possibilities of getting it. My prospective employer asked me if I would drive him to the airport. I said, "Yes," of course. The airport was about fifteen miles away, six miles through traffic and nine miles on the freeway.

We talked about the future of the city and how his company would fit into the directions of growth that seemed to be substantial. I seemed to be driving on automatic in the ebb and flow of late afternoon traffic because I was so involved in our conversation. I could not remember much of anything about the traffic in general or how fast I drove. My consciousness was devoted to our discussion.

I let the man out at the passenger departure area, and said goodbye and thanked him for such an informative interview.

The next day my prospective boss called to let me know that I did not get the job. He said that I had most of the qualities that he wanted for the person taking that position—intelligence, creativity, honesty, consideration—and he thought we would get along very well. But I was not aggressive enough.

I asked him how he determined that I was not aggressive enough. He said that in driving him to the airport I had been too considerate of other drivers, letting them change lanes in front of me, backing off when they entered the freeway, not going fast enough.

"But," I said, "I can do those things if that's what you want." He said I didn't do them unconsciously, and that was important to him. He had me drive him to the airport and kept me involved in conversation to find out what my automatic responses were. It's an interesting way to evaluate people.

After that interview, I looked at driving a little differently. Driving can be a helpful way for me to understand behavior and valuing in myself and others.

When I am driving, I can get upset, mad, irate, and downright angry, especially if I do something I don't really value. Often I rationalize about being in a hurry, or the other driver's lack of courtesy, or some such excuse. The more I am aware of my own incongruities, the more tolerant and mellow I become in regard to someone else's incongruities.

When other drivers care about me by letting me pass or blinking their lights when mine are on, I learn to care more about them.

Whenever I am an inconsiderate driver, I now seek to figure out why my actions failed to coincide with my values. Then I lose some of my "holier-than-thouness."

There are many more relationships between how one accomplishes a task, and how one lives life in general. Going on a camping trip is a valuable way to get to know yourself and others, often more telling than driving.

Every moment is new and fresh in an ever-changing environment when we are mindful and aware. In acknowledging all things, we can learn to accept all things. We cannot teach other drivers a lesson. We can only teach ourselves.

We can, however, let other drivers know what is possible.

Ideals are thoughts. So long as they exist merely as thoughts, the power in them remains ineffective, however great the enthusiasm and however strong the conviction with which the thought is held. Their power only becomes effective when they are taken up into some refined human personality.

—ALBERT SCHWEITZER

8

Wrong Way

If Zen is to become integrated into Western culture, it requires a Western idiom: "Chop wood, carry water" must somehow become, "Make love, drive Freeway."

—CHARLOTTE JOKO BECK

*A*s a kid, driving in San Francisco, I managed to go the wrong way on one way streets more than once. But, it was kind of fun. People tooted and waved. No one was going fast enough to do any damage, and at the end of the block, I would manage to turn off or turn around. But, as the country grew and I grew, I found that things could be more harrowing.

One warm summer evening, a friend and I met two more friends for dinner in San Rafael and then went to the Marin Community Center to listen to some wonderful speakers who expounded on VERY IMPORTANT things, I no longer remember what. When it was over, my friend and I followed our two other friends home in separate cars because we were going to spend the night with them in their new Sonoma home that neither of us had been to.

I'm a good follower and kept good track of my friends in the red car. After a right turn onto what

appeared to be a freeway on-ramp, I had a strange feeling, because the double yellow line was to my right,
instead of to my left.

At about the same time, the red car made a hasty u-
turn in front of some oncoming traffic. There was not
enough time or space for us to turn also. It immediately
occurred to us that we were going the wrong way on a
two lane freeway off-ramp, instead of on-ramp.

Headlights appeared in both oncoming lanes.
Fortunately my friend yelled, "Blink your lights!" which I
did. Also, fortunately, most of these oncoming cars had
slowed to around 50 mph instead of 70 mph.

Four cars coming at us in our lane (their lane) managed to dodge us. Then there was a little space to do an
unbelievably fast u-turn. We made it and finally got off
the freeway ramp.

Our friends were parked and waiting for us at the
first stop sign, holding their breath and their ears, hoping
to not hear any loud crashing sounds.

Lucky? Crazy? Karma?

Being in the present moment often makes things go in
slow motion. It seemed like hours when we were stuck in

that off-ramp, when it was probably only seconds. The other people on that ramp were my teammates. We were all on the same team in cooperation, not competition. Their interconnectedness saved us all. We were not separate, but ONE using our capabilities in interaction and harmony.

After that episode, I wanted to find a way to attach a neon sign on the top of my car, a sign that blinked a big "Thank You" to such interrelated people. One friend was concerned that if I were to find a way to do that, some others would manage to find signs that were considerably more negative.

The present moment is filled with joy and
happiness. If you are attentive, you will see it.
—THICH NHAT HANH

Not on my side of the street, Buster!

9

My First and Only Accident

*I think mainly Buddhism—the teaching of love,
kindness, tolerance, and especially the Buddhist
theory that all things are relative, is very helpful
when we are facing tragedy or a negative thing.
Since each thing is relative, there are
many different aspects.*

—THE DALAI LAMA

*A*bout thirty years ago, two friends were with me in the front seat of my Pontiac. We were heading for home after spending the weekend with more friends at a reunion in Chico. We were in the middle of the upper Sacramento valley, which is pretty wide and flat for miles and miles, and it was nighttime.

Far ahead were the headlights of a car approaching. After awhile, the lights disappeared. I didn't know if there was a bend in the road, or a hill, or if the other car had turned into a lane and gone home.

We were going up over a small train track incline when right in front of my face was the bright glare of two sets of headlights, next to each other, and one set was on my side of the road.

I braked and pulled to my right, but not so far as to tumble down the train track embankment. The extra set of headlights pulled to its right, but not so far as to crash into the set of headlights that were where they were supposed to be. We were about to hit head on, and I'm sure that before I saw the double headlights my car was going at least 65 mph. Since the other car was passing, it was probably going at a similar rate.

There was a whopping loud crash and a jerking around, and then nothing. I was badly shaken but seemed to be OK. My two friends amazingly were also unhurt.

I got out of the car and checked the other vehicle. Remarkably the driver was all right and so was his passenger, who had been asleep in the back seat.

Both cars were totaled, but every person was all right—not even a scratch! Cars were built more like tanks in those days, with more heavy metal. Maybe that's why we were so well protected. Maybe we all had good karma going into this situation.

It was amazing how soon, in the dead of night in the middle of nowhere, a police officer found us, and took care of all the details of getting the cars off the road and getting all of us to the nearest town. But it took about two years for the insurance company to reimburse me for the damage to my car.

I did not drive very much after that. I did not trust other drivers as I had in the past. Eventually, I learned how to enjoy driving again. I am now much more attentive to what other drivers are doing or can do when they are careless.

There is no birth or death, only continuation. When we look back at our own existence, we find not only a mother and father, but grandmothers and grandfathers as well as great-grandparents. We cannot change anything into nothing. It can change form but not disappear.

Many believe that to die means becoming nothing. But you can't make something into nothing. Energies can change form, but something can never become nothing.

Inner peace is the key. In that state of mind you can deal with situations with calmness and reason, while keeping your inner happiness.

—THE DALAI LAMA

When all else fails, use your turn signals.

10

Road Rage

*We shall know each other or
exterminate each other.*

—CARLOS FUENTES

This is an easy trap to fall into. No one else on the road drives the way you do and if you expect them to you will often suffer road rage. Even I must acknowledge having fallen into such a pitiful pit when I was younger.

Some people ARE inconsiderate, and that's their problem. But many drivers are just ignorant or beginners. Many are unaware that they have offended you, and it was feeling offended that made me want to crash into the offender, or at least give them a small but intense bump. Shooting them never occurred to me.

I can recall once when a little old lady in a large older car entered the freeway right next to me. The fast lane was too crowded to move into, and I had a bumper sitter right behind me. I have never been a honker, though sometimes it's the wisest thing to do. It would probably have given her a heart attack. So, I braked somewhat, not too much for the man on my bumper, but enough to keep her from side-swiping me.

Get a horse!

As soon as I could, I passed her, and as I put my hand up to shake my fist at her, I saw that it was a sweet little neighbor of mine. I was quickly able to change my hand to a wave and she smiled and waved back. She's the kind of person who is just not aware of much that is going on around her, especially when she drives.

On another occasion, a young man was weaving in and out of the right and left lanes, trying to get ahead of everyone on the road, without even signaling. I had spotted him in my rearview and premeditated a plan to upset his inconsiderate zig-zagging. He could wait patiently like the rest of us do while the slow person in the fast lane finally decides to move over. I crept up on the car in front of me until there was only about a car length between us—unsafe at any speed. I planned to keep him from zigging in front of me. He did it anyway. All he needed was a car length. I was furious. I became his bumper hugger as long as he stayed in front of me. But soon he was off zigging and zagging again, and I managed to refrain from joining him.

I had not slowed him down at all. I had totally failed in teaching him patience, and now I was struggling with high adrenaline, high blood pressure, and anger. I did this to myself. I just used him as an excuse.

One of the problems here is the need for communication. I will gladly let people move about the freeway all they want if they will let me know what they want to do. And I hope they will do the same for me. Of course, it is not just courtesy and consideration. There is a lot of safety involved in letting those around you know what you are doing so they won't hit you. This is true even when you are walking down the street or reaching across the table for the catsup.

When we are angry, we need to learn to observe the anger with love and attention. If we get angry because we are angry, we will double the anger. When we acknowledge our anger without judgment, it will transform itself. Awareness of our feelings will not suppress them or drive them out. But mindfulness causes transformation because it is not judgmental.

How long have the planets been circling the sun? Are they getting anywhere and do they go faster and faster in order to arrive? How often has the spring returned to the earth? Does it come faster and fancier every year, to be sure to be better than last spring, and hurry on its way to the spring that shall outspring all springs?
—ALAN WATTS

11

Freeway
Oneness-ism

The next time you are caught in a traffic jam,
don't fight it. It's useless to fight. Sit back and
smile to yourself, a smile of compassion and
loving kindness. Enjoy the present moment,
breathing and smiling, and make the other
people in your car happy.

—THICH NHAT HANH

In some ways, urban freeway driving is much more difficult than rural highway driving. There are so many more cars, and so many more lanes, and so many more signs. There are on-ramps and off-ramps. There are additional lane merges and there are removal of lane merges. There are accident merges and slow-downs for strange and unusual views. There are speed-balls and slowballs and inconsiderateballs. In some ways there are almost too many things happening at once.

Because there is so much happening, it consumes me. I am not about to let my mind wander. I have no problem listening to people in the car with me. I just don't listen at all. My friends know they can tell me their deepest secrets when I am driving and they will be safe with me forever. Sometimes music on the radio seeps in, but not much.

I am totally driving. All of me is enmeshed in cal-culating speed, extending my right foot on the gas pedal or the brake, exerting pressure on the steering wheel in order to change lanes or to take road curvature into account. I am aware of the road conditions involving wetness, dryness, or slickness, the closeness and nearness of cars to my right and left, in front and behind. I am aware of how fast cars come up behind me, how close they get before they slow down, whether they are inclined to pass me on the right or the left or just stay put. I pay attention to which lane line, right or left, cars tend to drift toward, especially when I am anticipating passing them.

I take note of lapses in attention in the drivers around me. I try to figure out if they are due to an unusual event like changing radio or tape venues, or if they are a part of the drivers' lack of training or mental condition, so that I should know whether to expect more lapses or not.

Sometimes I check to see how fast I am going in relation to the traffic flow. Sometimes we are all going very fast. Sometimes very slow. Sometimes I wonder if I am going faster than that Honda ahead of me or not. Should I pass or just follow?

In the old days when commuting to work, I drove on automatic and used my car time for analyzing the problems confronting me in my job, or sometimes the problems confronting me in my private life. What could I have said that would have been more appropriate? What could I have done differently? I thought I was being efficient in my use of time. When I discovered that I did not possess time, but that time possessed me, I began to change.

Sometimes I forget where I am going because I get hypnotized by all the incoming stimuli and the drama that is playing out before me. Sometimes I don't realize I should have turned off three miles back. Such a small price to pay for total immersion in a fascinating game that takes my mind off all my troubles. I am much more refreshed than when I keep reviewing problems over and over again.

Love cannot exist if it arises out of fear or guilt, and not out of understanding. You cannot love someone you do not understand. If you believe you love, but do not understand, it is not love. It is something else.

Unless peace is made by those who are peaceful, there will be no peace. When we produce peace and happiness in ourselves, we begin to produce peace and happiness everywhere.

*For what we call "nature" is free from a certain
kind of scheming and self-importance. The birds
and beasts indeed pursue their business of eating
and breeding with utmost devotion. But they do
not justify it; they do not pretend that it serves
higher ends or that it makes a significant
contribution to the progress of the world.*

—ALAN WATTS

12

Snow

*You can only live in one moment at a time, and
you cannot think simultaneously about listening
to the waves, and whether you are enjoying
listening to the waves.*

—ALAN WATTS

I heaved a sigh of relief after slowly creeping over the Mt. Lassen summit without having anything dreadful happen on this first snowy day of winter. I went down the first incline without difficulty. But on the second slope, I (the car and me) started sliding toward the right edge of the road and the ravine.

Before this I had no concept of such complete loss of control. Neither steering nor braking helped. I didn't think to try accelerating. I just kept sliding toward the ravine in utter amazement.

Then the car did it all by itself. It swung around in a complete circle and a half and slid down the road backward. It came to a sudden thunk when the back bumper hit the embankment on the non-ravine side of the road. I was still in complete shock at having had nothing to do with this miracle.

My hind wheels were stuck in a ditch full of snow so I just stayed there, grateful to be alive and in one piece.

Soon a snow plow came along and gave me a tug and I was on my way.

I have been immovably stuck since, on several occasions on icy roads, often at night, sometimes in the middle of a snow storm. Each time help has arrived within minutes, often from road crews, but sometimes from nice people who were willing to give me a tug.

When I did a lot of snow driving, I found a helpful solution to most of the problems of icy roads. I had an extra set of tires for the rear of my car that were studded snow treads. Every winter I would put them on the car and every spring I would take them off. They are better than chains because they aren't so hard on your tires or your car, and most of the time they are accepted in place of chains. They take much of the mystery and excitement out of snow driving, but they do help return some control to the driver.

When we are breathing, air moves itself in and out of our lungs. When we are seeing, light impinges on our retinas and makes us see. Sounds come to our ears without our seeking them out, as the wind blows and the water gurgles. We are carried along in time and space like a river that never flows out of the present.

The present is the only thing there is and the only thing that has no end. Without the capacity for living in the present there is no future, since when it arrives it will not be lived in its present moment.

To Taoists, freedom is understanding we are not in control and never will be. The only struggle is to stop struggling.

—WES "SCOOP" NISKER

减少开车

*I'm on the road less traveled
because I was mindful of
how I was driving, and not
enough mindful of where
I was driving.*

13

Automatic

*Every intelligent individual wants to know
what makes him tick, and yet is at once
fascinated and frustrated by the fact that oneself
is the most difficult of all things to know.*

—ALAN WATTS

$\mathcal{I}$ must admit it. I am not always a mindful driver. Sometimes I drive on automatic, too. So what I try to do is make my automatic as mindful as possible.

Whenever we learn something new, it is usually necessary to control our movements at a conscious level. When first learning to ride a bike, when first learning the waltz, when first learning to type, it was all conscious and very messy. Nothing was automatic.

Professional athletes spend their lives learning to have the best automatic reflexes they can develop. They learn consciously at first, and then after much practice, the cerebellum and the automation process take over. They learn to process automatically by refining their movements with conscious control. They learn to concentrate on what they are doing and do it better and better each time. Their automatic responses and ability improve with each opportunity to perform without conscious control.

And that is what mindfulness is all about. Concentration. Improvement. Doing it better and better. And we non-athletes can do it too. As we become better at our mindful driving we will develop more skilled automatic behaviors that will be available when our conscious is somewhere else.

The moment something does not go according to plan, consciousness will take over and work out the complications until the possibility to go on automatic returns.

If your conscious driving is not very mindful in the first place, you will not develop very good habits that are available when you want to think about something else. If you are mindful and learn with concentration, you will learn habits that prevent tight squeaks from happening in the first place. Your mindfulness will get you out of messy situations even if bad things occur when you are on automatic.

We are pretty good at analyzing how motors, and planes, and cars, and other mechanical or technological things work. We do less well analyzing how our bodies walk, talk, breathe, and think. And we are totally unable to analyze how to grow brains and hearts, bones, eyes, ears, and fingers. Yet our bodies know.

To be aware of life and experience as it is this moment means to eliminate judgments or preconceived ideas about it. We must learn to sense and feel our experiences as they are without expectation or force. We do not feel feelings. We feel. We do not think thoughts. We are thought. We do not hear hearing or see sight nor smell smelling. There is no experience of "you" experiencing the experience.

> *There is also the disadvantage of being so close to it that one can never quite get at it. Nothing so eludes conscious inspection as consciousness itself.*
> —ALAN WATTS

Chains required? I hate chains. No one's going to make me put on . . . .Eeeeeyiiiiike!

14

The Top of the Mountain

*Taking a path is different from driving down a
highway to work. A path has something personal
about it; it implies choice or even mystery. To
choose one path is to reject another. A path is a
meandering walkway—you do not rush or even
drive down a pathway. A path is not goal
oriented. A path is THE WAY ITSELF,
and every moment on it is a holy moment;
a sacred seeing goes on there.*

—MATTHEW FOX

*T*he first time it happened, I was driving on a two-lane highway near the Trinity Alps in a well-wooded area of Northern California. It was a rolling, gently curving road, and there was no other traffic in either direction. All at once, I became the car. I could feel my tires rotating on the pavement and a divine sense of union with the road. There was no conscious effort to turn the wheel or press on the accelerator, because I was the road as well as the car. I was the harmony of the car and the road. I was the melody of the universe. I was bursting with joy and a feeling of oneness. My body was totally aware of everything around me; the eucalyptus trees along the roadside, the manzanita bushes, with their dusty green leaves, the tiny cloud overhead, the clicketyclack of the tires, the purr of the engine, the smell of fresh air. My body was all these and so much more. My whole body smiled in this union as we floated along together through the forest and out into the sunshine. Words are totally inadequate to describe the unbelievable happiness I felt.

I am unable to achieve this ultimate unity when someone else is with me in the car. But when I am alone, and on a curvy road, and traffic is at a minimum, I reach Nirvana. This unbelievable feeling of compassion and acceptance and oneness is overwhelming.

Everything is so beautiful and so simple, so refreshing and invigorating. I actually get high on this relationship between myself, the car, the road, and the universe. I become an undivided individual embedded in my environment, accepting everything, expecting nothing. This is not an adrenaline rush or even an endorphin rush. It is oneness-ism and it lingers for months and years.

One of the joys that I assume resulted from driving to Nirvana was a gigantic cosmic experience which kept me in Nirvana for a long time, without the aid of a car. For me this experience has explained life and death, freedom and happiness, peace aned oneness-ism. I have never been the same since. This was a very awesome, humbling, profound experience. Everything was unified with everything. All became one. I became God and God became me and everyone and everything else. I felt infinite joy, beauty, truth, eternity, infinity. Having been lucky enough to be here at all, I would be here or somewhere forever.

Your experiences will be different from mine, but these are some of the feelings we will have in common.

The balance of nature in which we thrive indicates the stage of evolution of our planet, the aspects of harmony and conflict necessary for human development. The environment creates the organism as the organism creates the environment. Each life is, in a sense, the whole of the whole.

Many of us are ready to reach Nirvana in our own ways and times. This is just one path among millions.

The meaning and purpose of dancing is the dance. Like music, also, it is fulfilled in each movement of its course. You do not play a sonata in order to reach the final chord, and if the meanings of things were simply in ends, composers would write nothing but finales.

—ALAN WATTS

If you think education's expensive, try ignorance.

Bibliography

Beck, Charlotte Joko. *Everyday Zen: Love and Work.* San Francisco: HarperSanFrancisco, 1989.

Berger. K. T. *Zen Driving.* New York: Ballantine, 1988.

Boldt, Laurence G. *Zen and the Art of Making a Living.* London: Arkana, 1991.

Chodron, Pema. *Start Where You Are: A Guide to Compassionate Living.* Boston: Shambhala, 1994.

Dalai Lama. *My Tibet.* Berkeley, CA: University of California Press, 1990.

Fox, Matthew. *Creation Spirituality.* San Francisco: HarperSanFrancisco, 1991.

Frost, Robert. *Robert Frost: Poetry and Prose.* Edward C. Lathem and Lawrence Thompson, eds. New York: Holt, Rinehart and Winston, 1972.

Golas, Thaddeus. *The Lazy Man's Guide to Enlightenment.* New York: Bantam, 1972.

Kabat-Zinn, Jon. *Wherever You Go, There You Are: Mindfulness Meditation in Everyday Life.* New York: Hyperion, 1994.

Krishnamurti, J. *On Living and Dying*. San Francisco: HarperSanFrancisco, 1992.

———. *On Learning and Knowledge*. San Francisco: HarperSanFrancisco, 1994.

Maurer, Herrymon. *The Way of Ways: Lao Tzu/Tao The Ching*. New York: Schocken Books, 1985.

Nhat Hanh, Thich. *The Heart of Understanding*. Berkeley, CA: Parallax, 1988.

———. *The Miracle of Mindfulness*. Boston: Beacon, 1975.

———. *Peace is Every Step*. New York: Bantam, 1991.

———. *Present Moment Wonderful Moment*. Berkeley, CA: Parallax, 1990.

Nisker, Wes "Scoop." *Crazy Wisdom: The Saint, The Zen Master, The Poet, The Fool*. Berkeley, CA: Ten Speed Press, 1990.

Ryan, Joan. "A Shortcut to Enlightenment," in *San Francisco Chronicle*, Nov. 24, 1996.

Schweitzer, Albert. *The Wisdom of Albert Schweitzer*. New York: Philosophical Library, 1968.

Wagner, Jane. *The Search for Signs of Intelligence in the Universe*. New York: HarperCollins, 1991.

Watts, Alan. *The Book: On the Taboo Against Knowing Who You Are*. New York: Collier, 1966.

———. *Nature, Man, and Woman*. New York: Vintage, 1970.

——. *The Wisdom of Insecurity.* New York: Vintage, 1951.

Ywahoo, Dhyani, in Sandy Boucher. *Turning the Wheel: American Women Creating the New Buddhism.* San Francisco: HarperSanFrancisco, 1988.

Zen Master Dogen, "Actualizing the Fundamental Point," in Kazuaki Tanahashi, ed. *Moon in a Dewdrop.* San Francisco: North Point Press, 1985.

*C*larice Bryan was born in San Francisco, and has lived in California most of her life, so driving is very important. In addition to helping drivers in general and women drivers in particular, this book is a demonstration of the everyday application of the mindfullness aspect of Buddhism. Bryan has not always been a Buddhist. She received a B.A. from Chico State College, an M.A. from Stanford University, and her Ed.D. from the University of California, Berkeley. She has been a college professor most of her life, teaching such things as perceptualmotor development, body concept and analysis of movement, values and ethics, special education physical education programs, and spent many years teaching health, physical education and women's studies at Humbolt State University in Arcata. In addition to her interest in perceptualmotor development, she has published *The Physical Side of Learning* (1994), and is also a published poet. She has a great passion for swimming, badminton, and Buddhism. When she is not on the freeway, she is working on her next book, *Divergent Universes,* a science fiction novel, or playing with her five cats and three pygmy goats.